MATH Word Problems Made Easy

Grade 6

by Jill Safro

NEW YORK • TORONTO • LONDON • AUCKLAND • SYDNEY
MEXICO CITY • NEW DELHI • HONG KONG • BUENOS AIRES

Teaching Resources

Cover design by Maria Lilja
Interior design by Holly Grundon
Interior illustrations by Mike Moran

ISBN 0-439-52974-3
Copyright © 2005 by Jill Safro
All rights reserved.
Printed in the U.S.A.

2 3 4 5 6 7 8 9 10   40   12 11 10 09 08 07 06 05

CONTENTS

Introduction 4

The Fantastic Five-Step Process 6

The Amazing Eight Strategies 9

   (1) Choose an Operation 10

   (2) Guess and Check 12

   (3) Draw a Picture 14

   (4) Make a List, Table, or Chart 16

   (5) Identify Too Much or Too Little Information 18

   (6) Find a Pattern 20

   (7) Use Logical Reasoning 22

   (8) Work Backward 24

The Happy Hundred Word Problems 26

   Number and Operations 27

   Algebra 55

   Geometry and Measurement 64

   Probability 71

   Reasoning 72

Answer Key 77

INTRODUCTION

When it comes to ranking math skills, problem solving is on top of the list. Literally. It's number one on the process standards listed in the *Principles and Standards for School Mathematics* (NCTM, 2000). According to the National Council of Teachers of Mathematics (NCTM), "*Problem-solving should be the central focus of all mathematics instruction and an integral part of all mathematical activity.*" In other words, problem solving is what math is all about.

When learning to read, we learn to recognize the letters of the alphabet, we practice letter–sound relationships, and we learn punctuation. But the goal is to eventually read text. The same goes for math. We learn how to recognize and write numerals, decipher symbols, determine numerical order, and work with operations like addition and subtraction. But what matters most is what we can do with these skills—applying what we know to solve problems in daily life.

Math Word Problems Made Easy: Grade 6 is designed to help you help students sharpen their problem-solving abilities (and share a chuckle or two along the way). This book is divided into three main sections to help you:

The Fantastic Five-Step Process

The first section describes a simple five-step problem-solving process and an introductory lesson you can share with your students. This process can be used with every math word problem they might encounter. This is a valuable concept to introduce at the beginning of the year and practice with students so that they will have an approach they can rely on as they encounter various types of problems throughout the year.

The Amazing Eight Strategies

Section two takes a look at the different types of problems students might encounter and describes eight strategies to consider when solving them. We discuss each strategy and provide sample problems (and solutions) so students can practice and master the strategy. You may want to introduce a new strategy every week, so that students will be thoroughly familiar with all the basic strategies and have had practice with them by the end of the second month of the school year.

The Happy Hundred Word Problems

Here you'll find 100 word problems that focus on math concepts specific to sixth grade. They're all written so students will find them interesting and fun.

The problems are arranged by mathematical standards. There are sections for Number and Operations, Algebra, Geometry, Measurement, Probability, and Reasoning. The problems are printed two to a page, leaving plenty of room for students to show their thinking. Use the problems to introduce concepts, practice strategies, or as an end point to check for understanding.

Learning a consistent problem-solving approach, becoming familiar with and practicing effective problem-solving strategies, and applying these ideas in word-problem contexts help students become more effective problem solvers and mathematicians. And with *Math Word Problems Made Easy: Grade 6*, they just might enjoy themselves while doing so.

The Fantastic Five-Step Process

What do you do when you first encounter a math word problem? This is what we need to help students deal with. We need to help them develop a process that they can use effectively to solve any type of math word problem. The Five-Step Process will help students *organize* their interpretation of and thinking about word problems.

The best way to help students understand the process is to demonstrate how to use it as you work through a problem on the board or overhead. Make a copy of the graphic organizer below. You can blow this up into a poster or provide each student with his or her own copy to refer back to as you bring students through this introductory lesson.

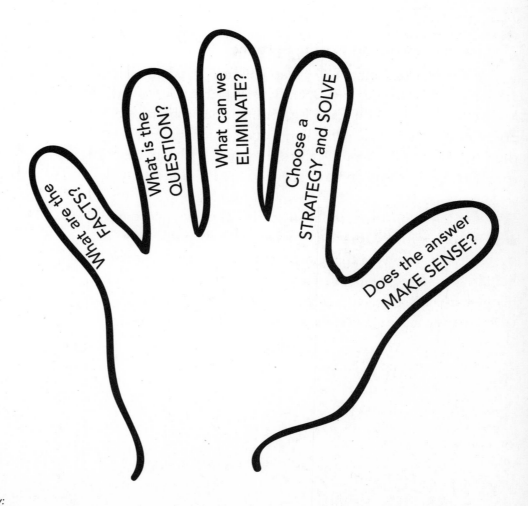

What are the FACTS?

What is the QUESTION?

What can we ELIMINATE?

Choose a STRATEGY and SOLVE

Does the answer MAKE SENSE?

Step 1: What Do We Know?

Begin by writing this problem on the board or overhead.

> Every year, Wienerville, Wisconsin, has a hot dog–eating contest. This year, there were four contestants. Little Frankie Footer ate 58 dogs. His brother Benny ate 3 times as many. Their friend, Phyllis, ate 180. Her brother Doug didn't eat any. Benny says he won the contest. Did he? How many dogs did he devour?

Read the problem carefully. What are the facts? Have students volunteer these orally. Write them on the board.

> Frankie Footer ate 58 hot dogs.
> Benny ate 3 times as many as Frankie.
> Phyllis ate 180 hot dogs.
> Doug didn't eat any.

Encourage students to write down the facts. This will help them focus on what is important while looking for ways to put it in a more accessible form. Can we arrange the facts in a way that will help us understand the problem situation? For instance, maybe it would be helpful to draw what we know, or put it in a list, or make a table. Sometimes it's helpful to arrange numbers from lower to higher or higher to lower, especially if we are asked to compare.

Step 2: What Do We Want to Know?

What is the question in the problem? What are we trying to find out? It is a good idea to have students state the question and also determine how the answer will be labeled. For example, if the answer is 180, then 180 what? 180 pumpkins? 180 fish? In this case, it's hot dogs.

> We want to know two things:
> 1. Did Benny win the contest?
> 2. How many hot dogs did Benny eat?

Step 3: What Can We Eliminate?

Once we know what we're trying to find out, we can decide what is unimportant. You may need all of the information, but usually there is some extra information that can be put aside.

> We can eliminate the fact that Doug didn't eat any hot dogs. Obviously he didn't win the contest.

Step 4: Choose a Strategy or Action and Solve

Is there an action in the story (for example, something being taken away or shared) that will help decide on an operation or a way to solve the problem?

> Since we know that Benny ate 3 times as many as Frankie, we need to multiply Frankie's total (58) by 3:
>
> $$58 \times 3 = 174$$
>
> Benny ate 174 hot dogs! That's less than Phyllis's 180. He lost the contest, because 180 is a greater number than 174.

Step 5: Does My Answer Make Sense?

Reread the problem. Look at the answer. Is it reasonable? Is it a sensible answer given what we know?

> It makes sense. 180 is higher than 174, and 174 is higher than 58. If the product was lower than 58, that would be a problem because the product of two positive numbers cannot be lower than the multiplicand.

Try a few different word problems using this "talk through" format with students. You can use sample problems from this book. Ask students to take a stab at the problem themselves first, and then do the step-by-step process together. Practicing the process in this way helps make it a part of a student's way of thinking mathematically.

The Amazing Eight Strategies

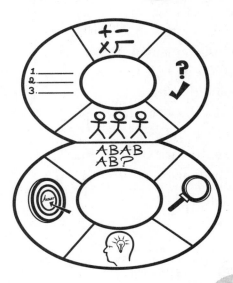

While we should encourage the use of the Five-Step Process to approach any problem, Step 4 (Choose a Strategy or Action and Solve) includes a wide range of choices. Some common strategies that are helpful to teach and practice are listed on the next few pages, along with sample problems. Students should have experience with all of the strategies. The more practice they have, the easier it is for them to choose a strategy that fits the problem and helps deliver an answer.

Tip

As students learn about and practice using these strategies to solve problems, ask them to create their own word problems. You can list the math concepts you want them to use in the problems (such as multiplication or fractions) and even the strategy that must be used to solve it. Students use these parameters to create their own problems, which they can share and try out with one another. As students begin to play with these elements, their knowledge of how problems work grows, as does their confidence when encountering new problems.

Choose an Operation

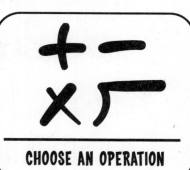

CHOOSE AN OPERATION

Even the most straightforward problem requires a mathematical operation to solve it. The question is, which one? After examining the information presented in a problem, students must decide which operation (addition, subtraction, multiplication, or division) they should use to solve it. Instruct them to read the problem and look for key words and phrases, such as "all together" or "more than" that may help move them in the right direction when choosing an operation. Then have them write an actual equation and solve.

SAMPLE PROBLEM

Uncle Otto ate a whole pumpkin pie in 21 minutes flat. Cousin Orville ate a whole pie in $\frac{1}{3}$ of that time. How long did it take Orville to eat the pie?

Solution

Otto ate the pie in 21 minutes. Orville's time was $\frac{1}{3}$ of that. One operation we could use to figure out Orville's time is division. With the information in the problem, we can create an equation:

$$21 \div 3 = ?$$

Answer: It took Orville 7 minutes to eat the whole pie.

SAMPLE PROBLEMS

1. Omar found 56 cents under a couch cushion! He lost half through a hole in his pocket. How much did Omar lose?

2. Villesville, Virginia, was founded on November 18, 2004. In what year will it celebrate its bicentennial (that's its 200th birthday!)?

3. Speedy Spotty can run a mile in 33 minutes. Fiesty Fido can do it in   the time. How long does it take Fido to finish a mile-long run?

4. The Micro Motel is the tallest tower in Tiny Town. It's 10 times taller than Tony's Tiny Trumpet Store. Tony's store is 2 inches tall. How tall is the Micro Motel?

ANSWERS

1. 28 cents (subtraction)

2. 2204 (addition)

3. 11 minutes (division)

4. 20 inches tall (multiplication)

STRATEGY 2:
Guess & Check

GUESS & CHECK

If you're not sure how to tackle a word problem, begin with a reasonable guess to get you started. Urge students to apply their estimation skills. This is the key to making a "reasonable" guess. Even just this first step is worth practicing. Then when a first attempted answer is arrived at, consider whether the answer is reasonable, too high, or too low. This is the "check" part of Guess and Check.

After considering the answer, have students decide if they need to revise and if so, how. Would a higher answer make sense? A lower answer? Try the following problem on the board and think aloud through the steps. Discuss the problem with students as you decide on your first attempt. Explain why you chose that number and how you are examining the number to determine if it is reasonable. Talk about how you are adjusting your initial attempt and why.

SAMPLE PROBLEM

Penelope Pig is eating her way through Cooter's Candy-Coated Bugs Shop. When she got there, there were two $5.25 chocolate-covered centipedes on the display shelf. There were also ten $2 caramel-coated spiders and six $1.50 cockroaches dipped in white chocolate. Penelope eats all but 3 of the candy-coated bugs. The 3 bugs are worth $8.25. What's left?

Solution

According to the problem, Penelope ate all but $8.25 worth of bugs and only 3 bugs were left.

Let's say one of each kind of bug is left: $5.25 + $2 + 1.50 = $8.75. The sum is too high! It seems reasonable that one of the bugs left is the centipede ($5.25) because its price will get us close to the desired total. We know that the other two bugs must be the same kind. What would give us the difference between the $8.25 total and the $5.25 centipede?

Let's try the cockroaches: $5.25 + $1.50 + $1.50 = $8.25 The answer checks out. Penelope did not eat 1 centipede and 2 cockroaches.

SAMPLE PROBLEMS

1. The new rock sensation, U3, is having a concert at Video City Music Hall. The orchestra section holds 4,730 people. The mezzanine section holds 6,713 people, while the balcony holds 8,444 people. The section behind the stage holds 10,472 people. In all, 23,646 fans attended the concert. They filled three whole sections. Which section of Video City Music Hall was empty for the concert?

2. Crafty Corey is making costumes for the new play, *Bugs on Broadway*. It stars the same number of 8-legged spiders as it does 100-legged centipedes. Corey's costumes have a total of 10,800 legs. How many spiders are in the show?

3. Shirley Shopper filled her basket with presents for Percy. She had a diamond-studded baseball cap for $8,163.17; a diamond-studded fishing pole for $9,014.01; a diamond-studded bowling ball for $10,743.86; and a diamond-studded diamond for $8,499.04. At the last minute, she put one of the items back on the shelf. In all, she spent $27,406.07 on Percy's presents. Which item did she put back?

4. Ira challenged Irving to a contest: If he could eat a 31-pound potato, a 21-pound pumpkin, a 19-pound tomato, and an entire 25-pound piece of cheese, Ira would give him his 1972 station wagon. Unfortunately, Irving ate only 3 of the items, for a total of 75 pounds. Which one did Irv NOT eat?

ANSWERS

1. The mezzanine was empty.

2. 100 spiders

3. The fishing pole

4. The pumpkin

STRATEGY 3:
Draw a Picture

DRAW A PICTURE

Drawing a picture can help answer the question, "What do we know?" Sometimes words do not easily convey the facts. Sometimes they can even confuse. By having students draw what they know, the problem can become clearer, the facts more easily manipulated, and relationships more quickly discovered.

When students use drawings or diagrams to help solve problems, remind them to use simple symbols to represent elements in a problem, such as stick figures for people. Unnecessary details or coloring should be left out.

SAMPLE PROBLEM

If there's one thing the Frost family enjoys, it's building snowmen. Today, they built 12! They put black hats on half of the snowmen. One third of the snowmen got red hats. After that, the Frosts ran out of hats. So the rest are wearing wigs. How many snowmen are wearing wigs?

Solution

Answer: 2 snowmen are wearing wigs

SAMPLE PROBLEMS

1. Randy the roofer finished 6 roofs today. Unfortunately, he was hired to do 14! Half of the unfinished roofs are covered in blue plastic. One-fourth of the unfinished roofs are covered in red plastic. And the rest are covered in polka-dotted plastic. How many roofs are covered with polka dots?

2. Carrie's head is full of curlers. There are 16 in all. One-fourth of the curlers are pink. There are twice as many green curlers as pink ones. The rest are soda cans. How many cans are on Carrie's head?

3. Morey mowed half of Mickey's lawn. Matty mowed $\frac{1}{4}$ as much as Morey did. Midge mowed twice as much as Matty. How much of Mickey's lawn has not been mowed?

4. Mr. Mozzarella's sixth-grade class is having a pizza party! Half of the pie is covered with peanuts. One-third of the pie has pecans. The rest has pistachios. How much of the pie has pistachios?

ANSWERS

1. 2 roofs

2. 4 cans

3. $\frac{1}{8}$ of the lawn is unmowed

4. $\frac{1}{6}$ of the pie has pistachios

STRATEGY 4:

Make a List, Table, or Chart

This strategy helps us identify and organize what we know. For example, in problems where combinations must be determined, listing all possible combinations is essential to see if students have considered all the possibilities. Setting up tables or charts can also help reveal patterns or relationships that may exist in sets of data.

```
1._____
2._____
3._____
   _____
MAKE A LIST, TABLE, OR CHART
```

SAMPLE PROBLEM

Peter Pumpernickel is hosting a party to celebrate Sandwich Appreciation Month. The cold-cut platter includes salami, bologna, and pastrami. How many kinds of sandwiches can Peter's guests make?

Solution

To solve this problem, students should make a systematic list to keep track of all the possible combinations:

1. salami

2. bologna

3. pastrami

4. salami and bologna

5. salami and pastrami

6. salami, bologna, and pastrami

7. bologna and pastrami

Answer: 7 possible cold-cut combos

Math Word Problems Made Easy:
Grade 6

16

SAMPLE PROBLEMS

1. Crafty Carla is dressing a scarecrow for her garden. She has 4 shirts (brown, green, blue, and pink), 2 kinds of pants (red velvet sweatpants and orange velvet sweatpants), and 3 hats (a baseball cap, a top hat, and a ski cap). How many different outfits can she make for the scarecrow?

2. Darius the doorman needs a new look. He has 4 hats (a beret, a captain's hat, a Statue of Liberty hat, and mouse ears). He has 3 types of shoes (slippers, flip-flops, and tap shoes). How many combinations of one hat and one type of shoes can he make?

3. The 6 members of the Beverly Hills Sandwich Appreciation Club are having a meeting. Each member will serve a sandwich to every other member of the club (but not themselves). How many sandwiches will be served at the meeting?

4. Holly, Carlyle, Sarah Jane, and Bryan are competing in the Fourth Annual One-Legged Race! They're now on the last leg of the race. How many different ways could they finish?

ANSWERS

1. 24 outfits

2. 12 combinations

3. 30 sandwiches

4. 24 ways

STRATEGY 5:

Identify Too Much or Too Little Information

In the real world, we sometimes encounter situations in which we have too much or too little information to solve a problem. The same goes in the math world. Often, word problems contain information that isn't needed to find the solutions. In this case, it's best to read the question carefully, then go back and focus on the numbers and facts needed to answer the question. Suggest that students cross out any irrelevant facts and numbers to simplify the word problem, if necessary.

IDENTIFY TOO MUCH OR TOO LITTLE INFORMATION

Other times, a problem may be missing key bits of information necessary to solve the problem. While such problems rarely appear on standardized tests, it's good practice for students to learn to identify what information they would need to solve such a problem.

SAMPLE PROBLEM

Doogie McDougal is whipping up 72 different snacks for his 12th annual Blooper Bowl bash. He invited 138 guests—but only $\frac{1}{6}$ are coming. That doesn't bother Doogie. He still makes 100 bowls of nacho dip. He makes twice as many bowls of chili. How many guests are coming to the party?

Solution

There is more information than we need to solve this problem. The question is how many guests are coming to Doogie's party. To figure this, we divide 138 by 6 (since $\frac{1}{6}$ of the invited guests plan to attend). **Answer:** 23

SAMPLE PROBLEMS

1. Darla won the dance marathon! She danced 3 hours longer than Danny. Danny danced 5 hours longer than Daryl. And Daryl danced 5 minutes more than Myrtle. Is there enough information to figure out how long Darla danced? Explain.

2. Horace bought 70 souvenirs at Stanley's Souvenir Shack at 1:15 P.M. Each souvenir cost $1.30 and weighed 17 pounds. He put $3.90 worth of souvenirs in his backpack and $6.50 worth in his briefcase. He put the rest in a wagon at 3:20 P.M. How much did Horace spend on souvenirs at Stanley's?

3. Patty Peters has two pools filled with prune juice. Pool One has 573 more gallons of juice than Pool Two. What information do you need to figure out how much prune juice Patty has in both pools?

4. It's feeding time at the Zanyville Zoo. That means its 10:12 in the morning! The zookeeper gives 600 candy apples to the 72 kangaroos. That takes 20 minutes. He throws 16 pecan pies to the 27 porcupines. That takes 15 minutes. Finally, he gives 837 peanut-butter sandwiches to 200 polar bears. That takes a total of 18 minutes. At what time does the zookeeper finish feeding these Zanyville Zoo residents?

ANSWERS

1. No; we need to know how long Myrtle danced.

2. $91

3. How much juice is in Pool Two?

4. 11:05 A.M.

Find a Pattern

Using lists and drawing pictures can help reveal patterns that may exist within the information a problem supplies. To discover patterns, ask: What relationships do you see between the numbers in the problem? How far apart are the numbers from each other? Do they increase or decrease by certain amounts in certain ways? Remind students that asking these questions will often lead to a good solution.

> **ABAB AB?**
> _____
> **FIND A PATTERN**

SAMPLE PROBLEM

Rusty spent $10 to mail a 10-pound watermelon to his Uncle Louie in Louisville. Rusty's brother Bucky spent $12 to send a 12-pound watermelon. It cost their sister Cindy $14 to send Uncle Louie a 14-pound watermelon. How much did sister Samantha spend to send a 20-pounder to Uncle Louie?

Solution

Notice how the dollar amounts in this problem match the weights of the watermelons mailed. The pattern shows that it costs a dollar for every pound of watermelon mailed. We can surmise that a 20-pound watermelon would cost $20.
Answer: $20

SAMPLE PROBLEMS

1. Tony the tap dancer practices 20 minutes every Monday. On Tuesdays, he practices tapping for 30 minutes. On Wednesdays, Tony taps for 40 minutes. If he continues this pattern, how long does Tony tap on Saturdays?

2. Gross Gus is so gross! He just burped, burped, sneezed, burped, burped, and sneezed. Then he burped, burped, sneezed, burped, burped, sneezed, and burped? If the pattern continues, what will he do next?

3. Chef Jeff is making a very special lasagna. The bottom layer is peanut butter. The next layer is cream cheese. Next comes a layer of jellybeans, followed by peanut butter, then cream cheese, then jellybeans. What is the next layer made of?

4. Pink, pink, purple, green, stripes, stripes, stripes. Pink, pink, purple, green, stripes, stripes, stripes, pink, pink, purple . . . What comes next?

ANSWERS

1. 70 minutes
2. Burp
3. Peanut butter
4. Green

STRATEGY 7:
Use Logical Reasoning

Logical reasoning is a way to help students organize data and use the process of elimination to solve problems. Logic boxes and logic lines (see page 80) are helpful tools for organizing facts and using the process of elimination.

USE LOGICAL REASONING

SAMPLE PROBLEM 1

Skippy, Steve, and Stanley are on their way to a family reunion. One is traveling by hot-air balloon, another by blimp, and the third by pogo stick. Who's on the pogo stick? Use these clues to figure it out:
- Steve is afraid of blimps.
- Stanley is afraid of pogo sticks.
- Skippy loves balloons.

Solution

From the clues, we know that Steve won't travel by blimp. Put an X in the logic box next to Steve under Blimp. Stanley is afraid of pogo sticks so put an X next to Stanley under Pogo Stick. Skippy loves balloons so put a check next to Skippy under Balloon, and X out Pogo Stick and Blimp. X out the rest of the Balloon column. If Steve isn't in the balloon or blimp, he must be on the pogo stick. **Answer:** Steve is on the pogo stick.

	Blimp	Pogo Stick	Balloon
Steve	X	✓	X
Stanley	✓	X	X
Skippy	X	X	✓

SAMPLE PROBLEM 2

The airplane was invented after the telephone and peanut butter. George Washington Carver invented peanut butter after Alexander Graham Bell gave us the telephone. Which invention came first?

Solution

To solve, draw a logic line. We know that peanut butter goes to the left of the airplane and that the telephone goes to the left of peanut butter. **Answer:** The telephone was the first to be invented of the three.

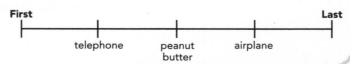

First   telephone   peanut butter   airplane   Last

$$9 + 7 = 16 + 4 = 20 - 7 = 13$$

SAMPLE PROBLEMS

1. Ignacious Whistlewhite invented an electric pinwheel (no wind necessary!). He invented it before he invented the glow-in-the-dark frying pan, but after the edible wallpaper. He invented an underwater television after the edible wallpaper, but before the electric pinwheel. What did he invent first? Use a logic line to find out.

2. Troy, Trevor, and Trina are the Trippety triplets. They're also super athletes. One is a world-class swimmer. Another is a medal-winning bicyclist. The third is a top tennis player. Who is the bike champ? Use the clues and a logic box to find out.
  • Trina needs a partner to play.
  • Trevor is afraid of water.

3. There are four U.S. states that have names starting with the letter "A." Arkansas has more residents than Alaska, but fewer than Arizona. Alabama has fewer residents than Arizona, but more than Arkansas. Which of the "A" states has the greatest population?

4. Zach, Zeke, Jere, and Jerry brought their pet cat, fish, dog, and snake to the vet for a checkup. But the vet's brand-new assistant mixed up all the animals. Use the clues and a logic box to help her figure out which pet belongs to who:
  • Zeke is allergic to cats.
  • Jere and Zeke are afraid of dogs.
  • Jerry loves to watch his pet swim all day.

ANSWERS
1. Edible wallpaper
2. Trevor is the bicycle champ
3. Arizona
4. Zach owns the dog, Zeke has the snake, Jere gets the cat, and Jerry owns the fish.

STRATEGY 8:
Work Backward

WORK BACKWARD

Working backward is a good strategy to use when we know how a problem ends up, but don't know how it started. The trick is to know where to begin and to think about using inverse operations.

SAMPLE PROBLEM

Donovan Doogle bought a bag of peanuts at the Dingaling Brothers Circus. He feeds half the peanuts to Elwood the elephant. Then he gives 4 peanuts to Marvin the monkey. Donovan eats the last 3 peanuts himself. How many peanuts were in the bag to begin with?

Solution

• To solve the problem, students can work backward. At the problem's end, Donovan ate 3 peanuts. Before that, he fed Marvin 4 peanuts. That's 3 + 4, or 7 peanuts.

• Before that, Donovan fed Elwood the elephant half of the peanuts. He had 7 peanuts after that, so he must have had twice as many peanuts before. That's 7 x 2, or 14 peanuts. **Answer:** The bag had 14 peanuts in all.

• Have students work forward to check the answer. See if the problem works if Donovan began with 14 peanuts.

$$9 + 7 = 16 + 4 = 20 - 7 = 13$$

SAMPLE PROBLEMS

1. Mervin Moneybags went on a spending spree today. He spent half of his money on a Slammy So-so baseball card. He spent $50 on a pair of puppies. And he blew his last $25 on a broken bike. How much money did Mervin spend today?

2. Anna finished the Walk-on-Your-Hands race in just 3 days! She walked one mile today. Yesterday, she walked 3 times the distance she walked on the first day. On day one, she walked 160 miles. (She spent the rest of the week applying hand lotion.) How long was the race?

3. Aunt Eloise wrote all of her Happy New Year cards in one day. She wrote $\frac{1}{2}$ of them while she ate a burrito for breakfast. She finished off 43 cards while she ate lima beans for lunch. And she did the final 57 while she devoured a doughnut for dinner. How many cards did Aunt Eloise write today?

4. Myron the muffin-maker made a special batch of huckleberry muffins this morning. He sold half the batch to Rudy the roofer. Then he sold 18 muffins to Bea the ballerina. He gave away half that amount to the Muffin Museum. And he ate the last muffin himself. How many muffins did Myron make this morning?

ANSWERS

1. $150

2. 641 miles

3. 200 cards

4. 56 muffins

The Happy Hundred Word Problems 100

The "Happy Hundred Word Problems" are organized by the NCTM content standards. Within each standard section, problems are further organized and labeled by the major math concepts typically found in sixth-grade math curriculums. For example, Number and Operations is a large standard that includes concepts like multiplication, division, fractions, and decimals. There are specific word problems here for each of these concepts. The answers are provided in the answer key on pp. 77–79.

As you introduce a problem, remind students to use the Five-Step Process. Keep the graphic organizer prominently displayed on a poster or chart, or give students a copy of their own to refer to. On each page you will find two problems with space for students to show their thinking. Encourage students to write down their solution process including any words, numbers, pictures, diagrams, or tables they use. This helps students with their thinking and understanding of the problem, while giving you more assessment information.

When assessing students' work on word problems, two major aspects need consideration: process and product. Observe students as they work on or discuss problems. Focus on what they say, and whether they use manipulatives, pictures, computation on scrap paper, or other strategies. When looking at their written products consider what skills they are exhibiting as well as what errors or misunderstandings they may be showing. This is why it is essential that students "show their thinking" as they solve a problem and explain their rationale.

Finally, have fun! These problems are designed to appeal to kids' sense of humor. Enjoy the situations and the process. Using what they know to solve word problems gives students a sense of mastery, accomplishment, meaning, and math power!

1 Whole Number Computation

The Bonks Zoo has a new mosquito exhibit. They have 475 Mississippi Mud Mosquitoes on display. That's 5 times more than the number of Boston Biters. How many Boston Biters do they have?

2 Whole Number Computation

Carlos has $60 to spend at the candy shop. He gets there at 8:50 A.M. He buys 12 gumdrops, 16 jumbo gumballs, and 6 two-pound jawbreakers. How many pieces of candy did Carlos buy?

3 Whole Number Computation

Jim Joseph Jinglehammer Smith is naming every star in the universe! He is naming them at a rate of 29,800 stars a year. He already has 350,000 names picked out. In how many years will he run out of names?

4 Whole Number Computation

Hanson and Grittle left their house with a basketful of pumpkins. To keep from getting lost, they dropped a pumpkin every 50 feet that they traveled. They dropped the last pumpkin at the 350-foot mark. How many pumpkins did they drop?

5 Whole Number Computation

Joanie got 732 jellybeans as a reward for cleaning her room. She gave half to Judy. Judy gave half of hers to Jessica. Jessica ate 13 jellybeans. How many does Jessica have left?

6 Whole Number Computation

Stella Steiner is having a stoop sale. She sold 6 times as many stoops from 3 to 5 P.M. as she did from 1 to 3 P.M. From 1 to 3 P.M., she sold half as many stoops as she sold from noon to 1 P.M. From noon to 1 P.M., she sold 8 times as many stoops as she sold in the morning. She sold 63 stoops this morning. How many stoops has she sold so far today?

7 **Whole Number Computation**

Warren Columbus sailed from Florida to New York. He tipped over every 255 miles. If the trip was 975 miles, how many times did he tip over?

8 **Whole Number Computation**

Rudy Rodin just finished a fabulous sculpture. In it, he used $\frac{1}{8}$ as many harmonicas as coffee cups, and 1,000 times as many pairs of sunglasses as he did coffee cups. He used 808,000 pairs of sunglasses. How many harmonicas are in the sculpture?

9 — Whole Number Computation

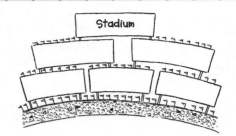

Hankee Stadium sells tickets one section at a time. The left-field section holds 17,134 people. The section in right field holds 10,444 people. The upper deck fits 15,777. The bleachers seat 12,001. And the section behind home plate holds 11,111. The Hankees sold exactly 37,332 tickets to yesterday's game. Which sections sold out?

10 — Whole Number Computation

Winnie the Witch is trying out a new spell. It calls for 33 ounces of salamander saliva. Luckily, she has 6 jars of it. Jar A has 17 ounces, Jar B has 8 ounces, Jar C has 15 ounces, Jar D has 3 ounces, Jar E has 22 ounces, and Jar F has 27 ounces. Winnie empties 3 jars, for a total of 33 ounces. Which jars does she use?

11 Whole Number Computation

Nervous Nigel woke up this morning and realized he was going bald. That realization caused 100 hairs to fall off his head. He lost another 179 on the drive to work. Another 232 hairs sprung off Nigel's head during a meeting with his boss. He lost 78 hairs while he ate his lunch. (Nigel finds meatloaf very stressful.) His last 37 hairs fell out when he looked in the mirror before going to bed. How many hairs did he start the day with?

12 Whole Number Computation

The Tooth Fairy is building a new castle—out of teeth! She figures she'll need 55,000,000 teeth altogether. If she collects 5,500,000 teeth a year, how many years will it take to gather enough teeth for her castle?

13 — Whole Number Computation

The *S.S. Rustbucket* is sailing from Newark, New Jersey, to Newark, Delaware. The crew has packed supplies for the grueling journey. Each crew member packed 88 chocolate bars, 72 granola bars, and 367 gumdrops. What information do you need to figure out how many gumdrops in all were brought aboard the *Rustbucket*?

14 — Whole Number Computation

Doctor Doo-alot is a very busy animal eye doctor. She has to give vision tests to 10 llamas, 172 porcupines, 76 seals, and 42 fish. If each vision test lasts 2 minutes, how many hours will it take the doctor to complete all the tests?

15 Whole Number Computation

New York Pets running back Sneaky Farber is quite the fumbler. He fumbled 7 more times against the Buffalo Bulls than he did against the Chicago Bores. He made 17 more fumbles against Chicago than against the Dallas Cowbells. He fumbled 6 times against Dallas. How many times did Farber fumble against the Bulls?

16 Whole Number Computation

Some people collect stamps—but Stewie Stevenson collects envelopes! He has half as many orange envelopes as he has blue envelopes. He has 14 more blue envelopes than green ones. He has 34 more green envelopes than polka-dot ones. And he just got his fourth polka-dot envelope today! How many envelopes does he have altogether?

17   Whole Number Computation

Thadeus's Thanksgiving feast was a major success! His guests ate the whole 70-pound turkey, 35 pounds of popcorn, and all 700 pumpkin pies. Everyone at the party ate the same number of pies. Is there enough information to figure out how many pies each guest ate? Explain.

18   Whole Number Computation

The fine folks of Waxville, Wyoming, made the world's tallest candle. They light it for a short time every day. As it burned today, it shrunk 100 feet more than it did yesterday. Yesterday, it shrunk half as much as it did the day before. And two days ago, it shrunk 500 feet. How much did the candle shrink today?

19 Whole Number Computation

Winnie the witch just got a new spell book—
*Quick and Easy Spells for the Overworked
Witch*. It contains 3 different spells that take
20 minutes each to complete, 5 spells that
take 9 minutes each, and 3 spells that take
4 minutes each. She performed 8 spells for
95 minutes. Which spells did she do? (She
didn't repeat any spells.)

20 Whole Number Computation

Aunt Edna is knitting hats for her
5 nephews. She wants each boy to get
2 red hats and 3 green hats. How many
hats does she need to knit?

21 Fractions and Decimals

Before Gus became a ghost, he had quite a few jobs. He spent 6 years as a waffle-maker, earning $6.25 an hour. He spent 17 years as a $4.25-per-hour doughnut delivery guy. And he put pepperoni pieces on pizzas for 38 years. He got a penny a piece. How much did Gus earn in a 7-hour shift as a waffle-maker?

22 Fractions and Decimals

55 cents apiece

Snyder's Spiders sells arachnids for $.10 apiece. Lulu's Ladybugs sells ladybugs for $.25 each. And Cora's Crawlies sells worms for $.55 apiece. Donald spends a total of $9 on exactly the same amount of each type of bug. How many worms did he buy?

FRACTIONS AND DECIMALS

23   Fractions and Decimals

Marvin and Minerva have 2 hours to spend at Howie's House of Horrors. They spend 16 minutes in the Hall of Howling Hooligans. They spend 27.5 minutes in the Laundry Room of Terror. And they spend 13.5 minutes in the Dining Room of Disaster. How much time do they have left?

24   Fractions and Decimals

It's feeding time at the Bonks Zoo. The monkeys get 6,000 bananas. The bunnies get half as many carrots as the monkeys get bananas. And the zookeepers get $\frac{1}{3}$ as many peanut-butter-and-jellyfish sandwiches as the bunnies get carrots. How many sandwiches do the zookeepers get?

25   Fractions and Decimals

Magico the magician has 6 volunteers from the audience. He plans to saw each one in half. And then he will saw the halves in half. How many pieces of volunteers will he have at the end of the trick?

26   Fractions and Decimals

Carlos is having trouble carrying all the candy he bought this morning. He puts half of it in a 6-wheeled wagon. He puts $\frac{1}{4}$ of it in his pocket. And he eats the rest. What information do you need to figure out how many pounds of candy Carlos ate?

Math Word Problems Made Easy: **Grade 6** (39)

27 Fractions and Decimals

Eloise Elderberry just got her weekly allowance. She put the whole $1.79 in the bank. At that rate, how much will Eloise have if she saves her allowance for two years?

28 Fractions and Decimals

Morey, Murray, and Francis all spent the same amount of time studying for the spelling test. (Francis and Murray failed.) If they spent a total of $16\frac{1}{2}$ minutes studying, how much time did each student put in?

29 Fractions and Decimals

Bruno is a blimp pilot. He earns $11.94 for every mile he flies. He earned 4 times as much on Saturday as he did on Sunday. And he earned $\frac{1}{16}$ as much on Sunday as he did on Monday. On Monday, he earned $3,056.64. How far did Bruno fly on Saturday?

30 Fractions and Decimals

Anna Fofanna went crazy at the Groomingdale's "After Groundhog Day" sale! She bought 4 designer wheels for her hamster, Huey. She spent exactly $69.57 on the 4 wheels. Which of the following did she NOT buy?

Moochie Wheel: $16.99
Roach Wheel: $13.45
Looie Baton Wheel: $27.00
Prouda Wheel: $43.08
Kat Speed Wheel: $12.13

31   Fractions and Decimals

On the second day of school, Edwina aced her first pop quiz of the year. Edwina spent 17 seconds on each of the first 77 questions and 16 seconds on each of the last 23 questions. In all, she answered $\frac{9}{10}$ of the questions correctly. How many questions did Edwina get wrong?

32   Fractions and Decimals

Wendell the weight lifter set a new personal record. He lifted 3 of the following 5 items: a 168-pound mailman, a 16.5-pound jar of jam, a 17.5-pound pair of clown shoes, a 125.5-pound case of coconuts, and a 175.5-pound rock. Which 3 items combined for a 317.5-pound lift for Wendell?

33   Fractions and Decimals

Stan and Fran are hosting a dinner party. Their marshmallow-meatloaf recipe serves 117. They invited 642 people to the party, but only $\frac{1}{6}$ plan to attend. Will Stan and Fran have enough meatloaf if they follow their recipe?

34   Fractions and Decimals

Fran wants to buy Stan a new outfit for their big dinner party. She picks out a plaid jacket for $19.97, a polka-dot beret for $6.99, and zebra-skin pants for $431.02. She has $450.39 in her wallet. Is that enough to pay for all 3 items?

35 Fractions and Decimals

Halloween is rough on the Tooth Fairy. It's her busiest season! This year, she collected 800,000 molars. She picked up twice as many bicuspids as molars. And she gathered $\frac{1}{4}$ as many incisors as bicuspids. What is her tooth total for this Halloween?

36 Fractions and Decimals

Dolly drank half a pitcher of clam juice. Her daughter, Darla, drank $\frac{1}{4}$ of what was left. How much clam juice was left after Darla was done?

37 Fractions and Decimals

The Tooth Fairy hired Chester Choppers to brush her castle (it's made of teeth). Chester makes $.25 a tooth. How much does he earn by brushing the whole 55,000,000-tooth castle?

38 Fractions and Decimals

The Tooth Fairy has decided to get the front of her tooth castle professionally whitened. Out of the 55,000,000 teeth in the castle, $\frac{1}{3}$ are in the front. How many teeth need to be whitened?

39 Fractions and Decimals

New York Hankee fan Lydia Vernon spent $148.50 at the concession stand. Which item did she NOT buy?

Hankee hat	$42.25
Hankee bobblehead doll	$30.25
Hankee magnet	$16.00
Hankee shirt	$60.00
Hankee hankie	$85.00

40 Fractions and Decimals

The Kooky Cookie Company is coming out with a new treat: cucumber-kiwi cookies! Each batch requires 17 tons of cucumbers. That's 34,000 pounds! It takes 2.5 times the amount of kiwis to complete the recipe. How many pounds of kiwis are needed per batch?

41 Fractions and Decimals

The president of the Kooky Cookie Company makes 12 cents for every chicken-chip cookie they sell. He makes $\frac{3}{4}$ as much for every tallbread cookie sold. For each quadruple-fudge cookie, he gets 5 times what he makes for one tallbread. How much does the president earn for one quadruple-fudge cookie?

42 Fractions and Decimals

Professor Plump put a 23.5-pound weight on one side of a scale and balanced it with 3 items on the other side. He had these items to choose from: a 4.5-pound rock, a 1.5-pound chunk of cheese, a 3-pound pumpkin, a 10-pound cat, a 6-pound book, and a 9-pound clock. What 3 items balanced the scale?

43   Fractions and Decimals

Doctor Doo-alot has prescribed a full set of contact lenses for Spencer, the 8-eyed spider. The final bill came to $400.80. How much did each lens cost?

44   Fractions and Decimals

Ivor, the ice-cream man, is preparing

12 cones. Half of the cones have 2 scoops,

$\frac{1}{4}$ have 3 scoops, and the rest have 1 scoop.

Half of the 2-scoop cones have sprinkles, $\frac{1}{3}$ of

the 3-scoop cones have sprinkles, and all of the

1-scoop cones have sprinkles. How many cones

have sprinkles?

45 Fractions and Decimals

Doctor Doo-alot speaks 3 different plant languages. Today, the doctor spent 2 hours speaking to daisies. He spent $\frac{1}{3}$ less time speaking to his pine tree as he did with the daisies. And he spent $\frac{1}{4}$ the time he gabbed with the tree chatting with the fern. How long did the doctor talk with the fern?

46 Fractions and Decimals

Pandora is painting the bottom of her pool. It's a pretty shade of pink! She paints $\frac{1}{3}$ of the pool before lunch. She paints $\frac{5}{6}$ of what's left after lunch. Then she runs out of paint. How much of the pool is unpainted?

47 **Fractions and Decimals**

Poor Peter lost twice as much money in May as he did in April. And he lost three times as much money in April as he did in March. In March, Peter lost $2,375.51. How much money did he lose in May?

48 **Fractions and Decimals**

Big Benny is the new burrito-eating champion of the world. He ate 2.5 times as many burritos as Large Lenny. Lenny downed 7.25 times as many burritos as Burly Bonnie. And Bonnie devoured 3 times as many as Tiny Tilly. Tilly ate 2 burritos. How many burritos did Big Benny eat?

49   Fractions and Decimals

Busby filled the bathtub so he could soak his aching back. One-fifth of the water splashed out when he stepped into the tub. Three times that amount splashed out when he sat down. How full was the tub for Busby's bath?

50   Fractions and Decimals

Winnie the witch has a new flying broomstick.

It uses olive oil as fuel. Winnie started the day

with $3\frac{3}{4}$ gallons of oil. By the end of the

day, she had used $\frac{1}{3}$ of the oil. How many

gallons of olive oil did she use today?

FRACTIONS AND DECIMALS

51 — Fractions and Decimals

Louie Libra finally balanced his antique scale. He placed a 67-pound pumpkin on one side of the scale. On the other, he placed 3 of the following items: a 27.5-pound turkey, a 26-pound bowling ball, a 22.5-pound paper weight, a 23.5-pound piece of chocolate, an 18-pound rock, and a 16-pound book. Which 3 items balanced the scale?

52 — Fractions and Decimals

Vito, the vendor, sells hot dogs at every Paramus Puppies game. One hot dog sells for $7.69. He sells an average of 23 hot dogs per inning. How much money does Vito make in a full 9-inning game?

FRACTIONS AND DECIMALS

53   Fractions and Decimals

Carmine ate half his candy bar. Then he cut the rest in half. He gave one half away and cut the rest in half. He gave half of that away. How much of the original candy bar does Carmine have left?

54   Fractions and Decimals

Pilar promised Paul $\frac{1}{2}$ of her pecan pie. Thurman gets $\frac{1}{3}$ of what's left. How much of the whole pie does Pilar give to Thurman?

55 Fractions and Decimals

Someone swiped the not-so-famous painting "Whistler's Uncle Joe" from the Museum of Mediocre Art! The guard discovered the theft today at 3:17 P.M. He called the police $\frac{1}{12}$ of an hour later. They caught the crook $2\frac{3}{10}$ hours later at a donut shop next to the museum. At what time did they make the arrest?

56 Fractions and Decimals

Matty bought 3 different items at the Snack Shack. He spent a total of $4.41. What did he buy?

Snack Shack Menu

Fried Olive	$.25
Fried Lemon	$3.05
Fried Lobster Lips	$.79
Fried Cantaloupe	$1.11

57 Algebra

Wanda wears purple for the whole month of March. In April, it's nothing but blue. May is maroon, and June is green. In July, she wears purple again. In August, it's blue. September has Wanda wearing maroon. If this pattern continues, what color does she wear in December?

58 Algebra

Doctor Peter Pawpaw is a podiatrist specializing in puppies and parrots. Today he examined the exact same number of each. In all, he checked 180 paws and claws! How many parrot patients did he see today?

59 Algebra

Master magician, Gary Goudini, has a bag full of beans. He pulls out a green bean followed by a pinto bean, a lima bean, garbanzo bean, garbanzo bean, green bean. Then it's pinto, lima, garbanzo, garbanzo, green, pinto, lima. If this pattern continues, what kind of bean does Gary get next?

60 Algebra

Cleveland, Ohio

Otis Owens loves to travel. He's already taken 10 trips this year. First he went to Cleveland, then Orlando, Kalamazoo, and Buffalo. Next he went to Orlando, Kalamazoo, Buffalo, Kalamazoo, and Buffalo. Where did he visit on his tenth trip?

61 Algebra

Beauford is on his way to his new school. His mother says it's only a hop, skip, and jump away—he hops, skips, and jumps the whole way there! If this pattern continues, what is his 32nd move—a hop, a skip, or a jump?

62 Algebra

Floyd is an Olympic hammer thrower. His first throw is 55 feet. His second throw is 52 feet, and his third throw is 47 feet. His fourth throw lands 40 feet away. Throw five lands 31 feet away. If this pattern continues, how far would his sixth throw fly?

63 Algebra

Beulah bought a brush for a buck. She paid for it with change. How many different coin combinations might she have used if she paid with at least 3 quarters?

64 Algebra

Apple, apple, pear, pear, apple, apple, banana, pear, apple, apple, pear, pear, apple, apple, banana, pear, apple, apple, pear, pear, apple, apple. What comes next in this pattern?

ALGEBRA

65 Algebra

Dashing Darwin has some dynamite dance moves. First, he does a split, then a spin, then a split, and a leap into the air. Then he does a split, a spin, a split, a leap, and a split. What would Darwin do next if he continues this pattern?

66 Algebra

Doctor Doo-alot treated an equal number of cats, parakeets, and fish today. In all, his 18 patients had 36 legs. How many fish did he treat today?

67 Algebra

Aunt Edna baked a 29-layer cake. The bottom layer is lemon flavor. On top of that, there's a layer of butterscotch. Then there's watermelon, chocolate, lemon, butterscotch, watermelon, and so on. If this pattern continues, what flavor is on top?

68 Algebra

Stripes, plaid, polka dots, stripes, stripes, plaid, plaid, polka dots, polka dots, stripes, plaid, polka dots, stripes, stripes, plaid, plaid, polka dots, polka dots. What comes next in this pattern?

69 Algebra

The I.E.W.P. (Incredibly Expensive Wireless Phone) Company just announced its new rates. At midnight, a one-minute call costs $.50. At 4:00 A.M., it costs $1 for a one-minute call. At 8:00 A.M., a one-minute call costs $1.50. If this pattern continues over a 24-hour period, how much does a one-minute call cost at 8:00 P.M.?

70 Algebra

Bertha loves bowling. She knocks down one pin with her first ball. (No one said she was any good!) Ball two hits 3 pins. Ball three hits 5 pins. The fourth ball topples 10 pins (strike!) and the fifth ball hits one pin. With the next three balls, she hits 3, 5, and 10 pins. If this pattern continues, how many pins would Bertha hit with the tenth ball?

71   Algebra

For Eddie's first birthday, his Aunt Edina gave him $3.79. She gave him $7.58 for his second birthday. And for his third, Aunt Edina gave Eddie $15.16. This year, Eddie got $242.56. Based on this pattern, how old is Eddie now?

72   Algebra

It isn't easy being a snowman in April. On Monday, Smedley melted 0.6 inches. On Tuesday, he melted 1.1 inches. On Wednesday, he melted 1.6 inches. If this pattern continues, how much will he melt on Friday?

73 Algebra

When Ollie was 3, he was 36 inches tall. At 4, he was 38 inches tall. By age 5, he was 41 inches tall. At age 6, he stood 45 inches tall. If this pattern continues, how tall will Ollie be at age 8?

74 Algebra

Roy is relaxing. He spends 17 minutes in a hammock. Then he floats in the pool for 29 minutes. He follows that with 42 minutes in the hammock. Next, he floats for 56 minutes. Continuing this pattern, how long will his next stay be in the hammock?

GEOMETRY AND MEASUREMENT

75   Geometry and Measurement

Ernie Erkoliani invented a battery-operated umbrella. The battery lasts 13 hours, 45 minutes per charge. Ernie turned it on at 7:02 P.M. and used it until 9:47 P.M. The next day, it was still pouring. Ernie turned on the umbrella at 6:21 A.M. and used it until 2:51 P.M. How much more time does Ernie have before he will have to recharge the battery?

76   Geometry and Measurement

The new supersonic speedy train is pretty amazing. It has a swimming pool! The pool measures 4 feet deep, 10 feet wide, and 15 feet long. How many cubic feet of water can the pool hold?

77 Geometry and Measurement

Otto is almost finished with his new photography book, *Noses of North America*. The book is in the shape of a right triangle—to look like a nose. The base of the book measures 9 inches. Its height measures 12 inches. What is the area of the book?

78 Geometry and Measurement

Hairy Harry's beard grew 5 inches in 2003. In 2002 it grew 15 centimeters. In 2001, it grew 0.1 meter. In which year did Hairy Harry's beard grow the longest?

79   Geometry and Measurement

Thadeus's Thanksgiving feast was just too much! He started cooking the 70-pound turkey at 11:00 A.M. At 11:30 A.M., he purchased 35 pounds of popcorn. He baked 700 pumpkin pies and half as many giblet-chip cookies. At 8:30 P.M., the turkey was finished cooking. His guests arrived at 6:00 P.M. They immediately ate $\frac{2}{3}$ of the cookies! How long did it take Thadeus's turkey to cook?

80   Geometry and Measurement

Crafty Carla is cutting her cousin Cora's tablecloth into 1-foot square napkins. The table cloth measures 9 feet by 9 feet. (Cora has a big table.) How many napkins can Carla make?

81   Geometry and Measurement

Farmer Phil planted a 1.25-mile row of apple trees. He planted a 7.50-mile row of plum trees. And he planted a 27.75-mile row of peach trees. How many kilometers* of trees did he plant?

* 1.6 kilometers = 1 mile

82   Geometry and Measurement

It's hard work being a 10,000,037-year-old ghost. Just ask Gus. He haunts the house at 423 Maple Street. He spends $\frac{1}{4}$ of the day rattling chains, 45 minutes a day opening and closing creaky doors, and 120 minutes a day moaning. How many hours does Gus spend rattling chains?

83 Geometry and Measurement

Farmer Fredo planted 18 acres of tiger lilies. He planted half as many acres of lion lilies. And he filled the rest of his farm with leopard lilies. He ended up with 3 times as many acres of leopard lilies as lion lilies. How big is Fredo's farm?

84 Geometry and Measurement

The Kooky Cookie Company is famous for its square cookies. Each one is 3 inches wide. How many cookies would it take to stretch a mile*?

* 1 mile = 5,280 feet

85   Geometry and Measurement

Howie's House of Horrors is 126 miles from Marvin and Minerva's beach bungalow. If they rollerskate at a steady rate of 2 miles per hour, how long will it take them to get to Howie's?

86   Geometry and Measurement

The New Jerkey Turnpike has a toll booth every 1.3 miles*. (It's free to get onto the road.) How many feet apart are the toll booths?

* 1 mile = 5,280 feet

87 Geometry and Measurement

Marty built a house out of 2-inch-square sugar cubes. The front of the house is 2 feet wide and 18 inches high. How many sugar cubes make up the front of Marty's house?

88 Geometry and Measurement

Brenda, Brandon, and Brendan are triplets. They were arguing about who is the tallest of the three. Brenda is 5 foot, 2 inches tall. Brandon measures 61 inches tall. Brendan stands at 1.6 meters* tall. Who is the tallest?

* 1 meter = 3.281 feet

PROBABILITY

89   Probability

Chef Stef is making today's Blue Plate Special. Each plate comes with a main dish, side dish, and a dessert. How many different combinations are possible with these options?

Main Dish
Meat Loaf
Tofu Loaf
Ham

Side Dish
Mashed Potatoes
Mashed Tomatoes
Mashed Lima Beans

Dessert
Carrot Cake
Cheesecake
Soybean Cake

90   Probability

Lil, Jill, and Phil are at the movie theater. How many different ways can they sit beside each other?

91 Probability

Kyle bought his kitten 3 new pairs of sneakers: a red pair, a blue pair, and a green pair. How many different combinations of new sneakers could Kyle's kitten wear?

92 Reasoning

Ernie, Bernie, Stanley, and Laverne brought gifts for Aunt Ethel's 80th birthday. One brought her a kitten. Another brought a yellow mitten. Another brought some salami, and the last brought a ping-pong paddle. Who brought what? Use these clues and a logic box to find out:

- Ernie and Bernie are allergic to cats.
- Laverne lost one of Aunt Ethel's yellow mittens.
- Ernie owns a salami store.

93 Logic and Reasoning

The National Marble League has ordered new uniforms for all of its teams: the Weehawken Wonders, the Moonachie Maulers, the Guttenberg Goons, and the Paramus Pounders. One uniform has polka dots. Another has a picture of a parakeet. One team wears pinstripes, and the last has a picture of a pair of pigeons. Which team has which uniform? Use these clues and a logic box to find out:

- Polka dots are illegal in Paramus and Weehawken.
- Guttenberg and Paramus have no birds on their uniforms.
- The parakeet is the official town bird of Moonachie.

94 Logic and Reasoning

It's snack time at the zoo. The giraffe, lion, elephant, and monkey are all enjoying a bite to eat. One is munching on a banana. Two are chewing on carrots. And the last is eating a bowl of cereal. Who's chomping on what? Use these clues and a logic box to find out:

- The monkey hates bananas.
- The lion isn't eating cereal or a banana.
- The elephant is using a spoon.

 **Logic and Reasoning**

The Shrimpson family is going to Carney Island amusement park. Burt, Lucy, Mildred, and Gomer each have a favorite ride. One loves the pirate ship. One can't get enough of the bumper cars. Another says the merry-go-round is number one. And the other loves the haunted house. Which ride is Mildred's favorite? Use these clues and a logic box to find out:
- Gomer hates rides that go in circles.
- Burt is wearing an eye patch and carrying a treasure chest.
- Lucy doesn't like rides that move.

 **Logic and Reasoning**

The Cow Television Network has announced its new Monday night schedule. *Who Wants to Be a Cow?* will be on before *The C.O.W.* And *Everybody Loves Cows* will be on before *Who Wants to Be a Cow?*, but after *The Cow of Queens*. Which of the shows will be on first? Draw a logic line to find out.

97 Logic and Reasoning

It's playoff time! Unfortunately, the New York Blankets, the Boston Toe Sox, the Arizona Diamond Rings, and the Minnesota Triplets won't be there. To get their minds off their stinky seasons, the teams are taking vacations. One is exploring New York. Another is vacationing in Boston. One is having fun in Arizona. And one team is seeing the sights of Minnesota. Which team stayed home for vacation? Use these clues and a logic box to find out:

- The Blankets are in the Southwestern United States.
- The Toe Sox are visiting the Statue of Liberty.

98 Logic and Reasoning

Ed, Fred, Ned, and Ted all have potato collections. Fred has more potatoes than Ted. Ned has more potatoes than Fred, but fewer potatoes than Ed. Who has the fewest potatoes? Use a logic line to find out.

99   Logic and Reasoning

It's time for the final race of the Snail Olympics. The American snail finishes before the German snail, but after the Irish snail. The Irish snail finishes before the French snail, but after the Swedish snail. Who won the race? Use a logic line to find out.

100   Logic and Reasoning

Murray, Minnie, and Molly Morton are at the Mama Meatball restaurant with their pet poodle, Pepper. They ordered a plate of fried chicken, a seaweed salad, a bucket of bones, and a chicken potpie. Who ordered what? Use the clues and a logic box to find out:
• Murray can't eat fried food.
• Molly is a vegetarian.
• Pepper hates chicken.

ANSWER KEY

Number and Operations

Whole Number Computation

1. 95 mosquitoes

2. 34 pieces of candy

3. He'll run out of names in year 12.

4. 7 pumpkins

5. 170 jellybeans

6. 2,331 stoops

7. 3 times

8. 101 harmonicas

9. Right field, upper deck, and home plate

10. Jars B, D, and E

11. 626 hairs

12. 10 years

13. We need to know how many members are in the crew.

14. 10 hours

15. 30 times

16. 120 envelopes

17. No. We need to know the number of guests at the feast.

18. 350 feet

19. 3 20-minute spells, 3 9-minute spells, and 2 4-minute spells

20. 25 hats

Fractions and Decimals

21. $43.75

22. 10 worms

23. 63 minutes

24. 1,000 sandwiches

25. 24 pieces

26. We need to know how many pounds of candy Carlos started with.

27. $186.16

28. $5 \frac{1}{2}$ minutes

29. 64 miles

30. Prouda Wheel

31. 10 questions

32. The jar of jam, the case of coconuts, and the rock

33. Yes

34. No

35. 2,800,000 teeth

36. $\frac{3}{8}$ of the pitcher

37. $13,750,000

38. 18,333,333 teeth

39. The Hankee hankie

40. 85,000 pounds of kiwis

41. 45 cents

42. The cat, the clock, and the rock

43. $50.10

44. 7 cones

45. 10 minutes

46. $\frac{1}{9}$ of the pool

47. $14,253.06

ANSWER KEY

48. 108.75 burritos

49. $\frac{1}{5}$ full

50. $1\frac{1}{4}$ gallons of olive oil

51. The turkey, the chocolate, and the book

52. $1,591.83

53. $\frac{1}{8}$ of the original candy bar

54. $\frac{1}{6}$ of the pie

55. 5:40 P.M.

56. A fried olive, a fried lemon, and a fried cantaloupe

Algebra

57. Blue

58. 30 parrots

59. Garbanzo bean

60. Buffalo

61. A skip

62. 20 feet

63. 13 different coin combinations

64. Banana

65. A spin

66. 6 fish

67. Lemon

68. Stripes

69. $3

70. 3 pins

71. 7 years old

72. 2.6 inches

73. 56 inches tall

74. 71 minutes

Geometry and Measurement

75. 3 hours

76. 600 cubic feet of water

77. 54 inches

78. In 2002

79. $9\frac{1}{2}$ hours

80. 81 napkins

81. 58.4 kilometers

82. 6 hours

83. 54 acres

84. 21,120 cookies

85. 63 hours

86. 6,864 feet

87. 108 sugar cubes

88. Brendan

Probability

89. 27 combinations

90. 6 different ways

91. 5 different combinations

Reasoning

92. Ernie brought salami, Bernie brought a ping-pong paddle, Stanley brought a kitten, and Laverne brought a mitten.

93. Weehawken has pigeons, Moonachie wears the parakeet uniform, Guttenberg wears polka dots, and Paramus wears pinstripes.

94. The giraffe is enjoying a banana, the lion and monkey are eating carrots, and the elephant is eating a bowl of cereal.

95. The merry-go-round

96. *The Cow of Queens*

97. The Minnesota Triplets

98. Ted

99. The Swedish snail

100. Murray had chicken potpie, Minnie got fried chicken, Molly ordered salad, and Pepper chowed on bones.

LOGIC BOX

LOGIC LINE